SUITE FOR STRINGS

VIOLIN I

Robert Washburn

I LITTLE MARCH

Moderate march tempo ♩ = 120

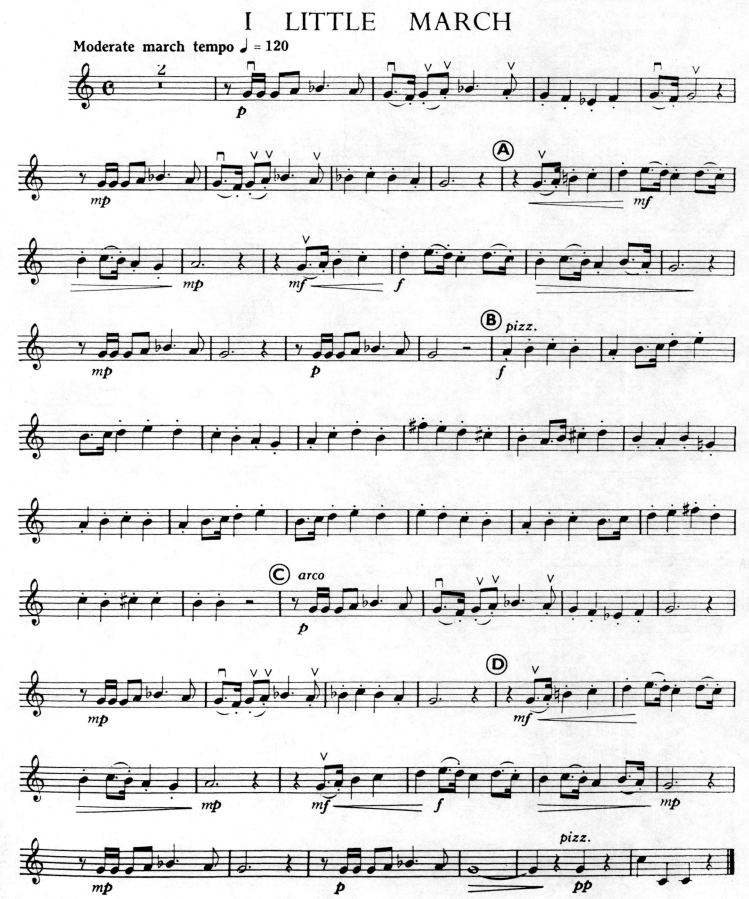

Printed in U.S.A.

OXFORD UNIVERSITY PRESS

II SONG

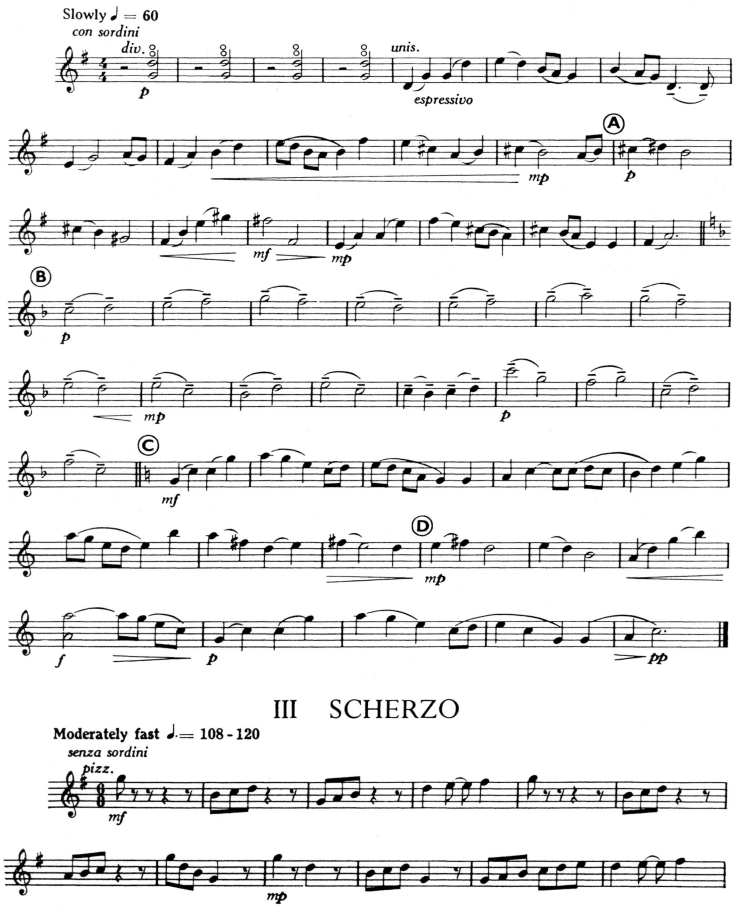

III SCHERZO

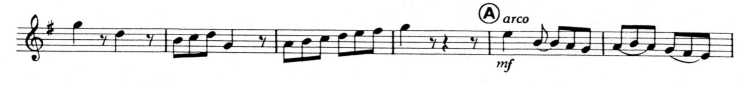
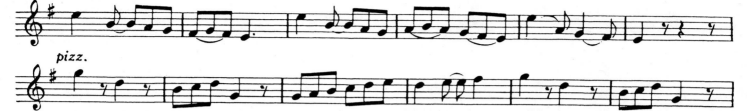
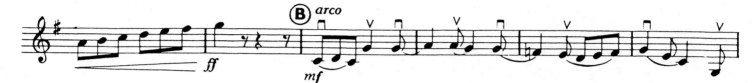
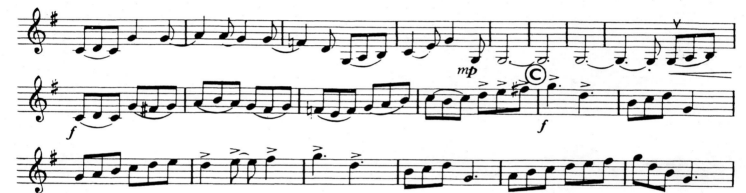
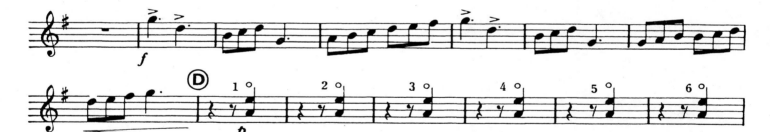
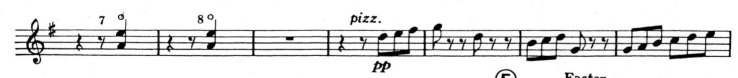
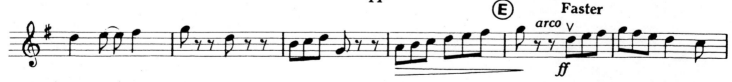
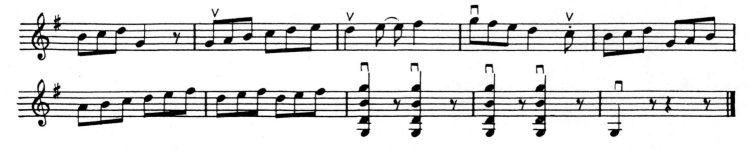

IV   FINALE

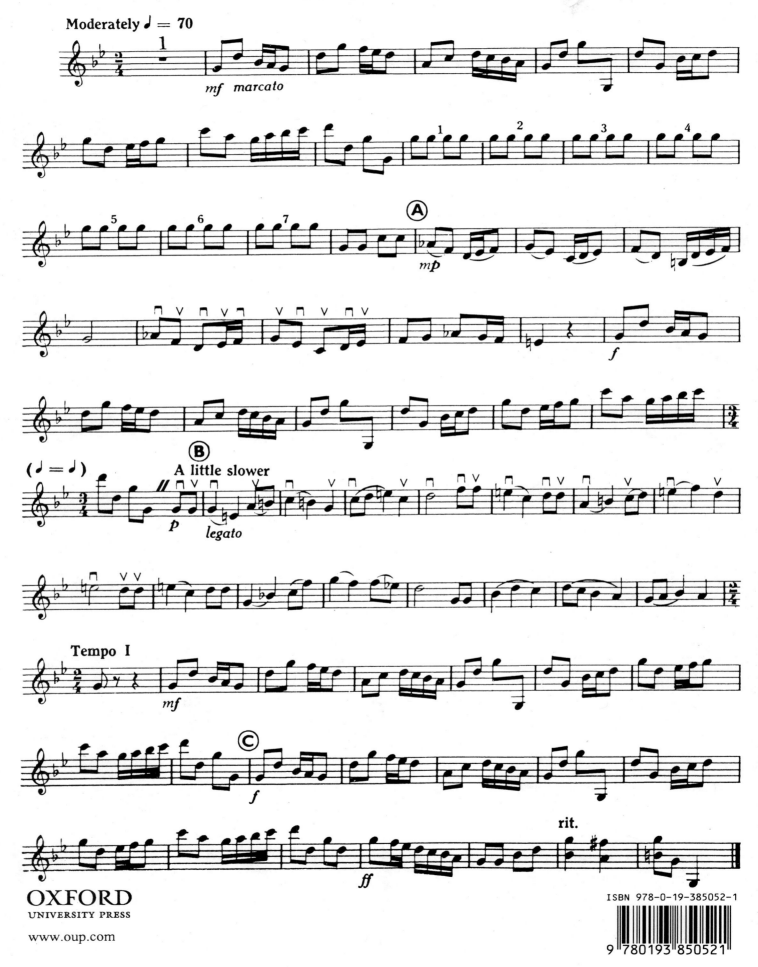

OXFORD
UNIVERSITY PRESS

www.oup.com

ISBN 978-0-19-385052-1

9 780193 850521